Social Media Ideas for Real Estate

Over 500 Content

Ideas to Post

(For Facebook, Instagram, Twitter, & More)

Danielle McCorkle

Social Media Ideas for Real Estate

Copyright © 2020 Danielle McCorkle

All rights reserved.

ISBN: 9798604404348

COPYRIGHT

Copyright ©2020 by Danielle McCorkle. All rights reserved. No part of this publication may be reproduced, stored in a retrieval system or transmitted in any form or by any means, electronic, mechanical, photocopying, recording, scanning, or otherwise, except as permitted under Sections 107 and 108 of the 1976 United States Copyright Act, without the prior written permission of the Publisher. No patent liability is assumed with respect to the use of information contained herein.

Trademarks: The One and Only Social Media Content Creation, Real Estate Edition are trademarks of the author and may not be used without written permission. All other trademarks are the property of their respective owners. The author is not associated with any product or vendor mentioned in this book. The publisher and author cannot attest to the accuracy of this information. Use of a terms in this book should not be regarded as affecting the validity of any trademark or service mark.

While the author has used their best efforts to prepare this book, they make no warranties or representations with respect to the accuracy or completeness of contents in this book and specifically disclaim any implied warranties of merchantability or fitness for a particular purpose. No warranty may be created or extended by sales representatives or written sales materials. The advice and strategies contained herein may not be suitable for your situation. You should consult with a professional where appropriate. The publisher and author shall not be liable for any loss of profit or any other commercial damages, including but not limited to special, incidental, consequential, or other damages. The fact that an organization or website is referred to in this work as a citation and/or a potential source of further information does not mean that the publisher and the author endorse the information the organization or website may provide or recommendations it may make. Further, readers should be aware that internet websites listed in this work may have changed or disappeared between when this work was written and when it is read.

Every effort has been made to make this book as complete and as accurate as possible, but no warranty or fitness is implied. The information provided is on an "as is" basis. The author and publisher shall have neither liability nor responsibility to any person or entity with respect to any loss or damages arising from the information contained in this book or from the use of any programs accompanying it.

Information and ideas have been obtained by the author. The author does not guarantee the accuracy, adequacy, or completeness of any information and is not responsible for any errors or omissions or the results obtained from the use of such information. All trademarks and copyrights mentioned herein are the possession of their respective owners and the author makes no claim of ownership by the mention of products that contain these marks.

CONTENTS

	Appreciation	i
1	Social Media	1
2	Social Media Statistics	Pg 9
3	Social Media Calendar	Pg 12
4	Creative Posts	Pg 18
5	Information for Clients	Pg 21
6	Listings	Pg 27
7	Tips	Pg 51
8	Content Posting	Pg 60
9	Your Business	Pg 67
10	Engagement	Pg 77
11	Resource Websites	Pg 79
12	More Content Ideas	Pg 81
13	# Hashtags	Pg 87

APPRECIATION

Thank you to all the hard-working people who work tirelessly every day to reach their goals.

1 SOCIAL MEDIA

Chances are you are a super busy person concentrating on your business and working on growing your business. Whether you post once a week, daily, or more than once daily, you need great content to keep visitors coming back to your social media network or networks. Sometimes you may run out of good ideas, not have the time to commit to posting, or not think of the ideas listed in this book. I hope this book helps you grow your business exponentially and helps your customers. Please keep in mind, these are ideas and you alone must decide what is best for your business and your social media strategy.

WHY SOCIAL MEDIA?

Why is Social Media Important to your Business?

#1 Reason: It shows everyone including potential customers that you are still in business.

Additional Important Reasons

Great content brings people back to your sites for more visits and it gives you more opportunities to increase your sales.

It adds validity to your business that you are an expert in your field.

It is a quick way to sell your business. In turn, it is also a quick way to turn away customers without a good social media presence and poor content.

It is a time-taking endeavor but it is free and a vital part of the business you want to grow.

Customers who view your social media decide if they want to spend their money with you.

It is a great free referral service. Your social media may be used by folks who are researching companies for their own use as well as to share with friends, family members, and colleagues.

The content you post should be in your words and they follow your social media goals.

Social media is the way many folks get informed locally as well as globally.

Your Social Media Goal(s)?

What is your social media goal

How are you going to accomplish this goal / these goals

How will each of your social media networks show your personality

Does your social media parallel your website

Set your goals with ways to use social media to boost your sales

How Often Should You Post?

How often to post depends on your business and your goals

Some businesses post daily

Some businesses post 1 time a week

Some businesses post every other week

Some businesses post as often as their competition

This is a decision that you need to make based on your business goals

What Should You Post About?

What is most important about your business and social media is that social media's purpose is to generate sales for your business.

Based on your business, experts recommend that you post a percentage of the time selling your products and the other percentage posting about non-selling content. However, you need to decide what is best for your business. If you are a restaurant, maybe you post 90 percent about your food with images. Maybe the other percentage is your business hours, your menu, when you are closed for any upcoming holidays. If you are a hair salon, maybe a larger percentage of your posts are about when you have open appointment times. If you are a real estate company, your posts may vary based on your listings. You may have a higher percentage of listing posts at different times throughout the year and the other times your posts are about your business, your community, your personality to reach more potential clients. Thus, it is your call regarding how often you post and about what.

One way to bring in customers and show that you are an expert in your field, is by posting frequently asked questions about valuable content that your customers and potential customers usually ask. For example, if you are a kitchen remodeling company, post articles with content about common questions customers may ask you. Some ideas may be about the different countertop materials available, painted vs stained cabinets, custom vs refaced cabinets, backsplashes, characteristics of different wood species, and more content similar to this.

Where does your content come from? You can either create your own content or include links to great content. Be sure to follow the legal rules for copyright, trademark, and other laws. It is very important to know the law regarding what you can and cannot as well as how to legally post.

Posting Content For Your Business

Let your posts show your business's personality

Post fun things about your business or your community

Post quotes or motivational messages

Post fun content that makes you chuckle

Drive your own narrative in your posts

Post what you are passionate about

There Are Different Ways To Post

Do you have a lot of words and information in the post or is it one to two sentences?

Do include your phone number, address, and company URL?

Do you add emojis?

Do you add other URLs?

Do you add hashtags?

Do you add other links to your other social media networks?

Are you incorporating other new ways to post on social media that is not available at the time this book was published?

Most important is the content that you are posting and the image(s) you use. Everything else is used to continue to generate sales and customers as well as potential customers visiting or sharing with others. Hopefully your content generates repeat visits, shares, and telling others to look at your social media posts.

Importance Of Images

Social media networks are very visual. It is important to have good images to draw in customers or potential clients to your business. Clear images are super important. Make sure you use the current optimal size for posting images. With the correct image sizes, you will be able to create engaging images that sends a message about your brand, services, products, and business goals. Since the shape and dimensions with social media networks changes, you need to research the current upload sizes.

There are many graphic design companies that have online graphic-design tools for free or for a charge. These are awesome drag and drop formats that are formatted for the social media network you want to create an image for. Perfect for non-designers and busy business people.

SOCIAL MEDIA'S PURPOSE AND REASON

The purpose of social media is to grow your business not put it out of business.

MAYBE DON'T POST ...

Don't repeat posting the same website's articles even if they are very good, mix it up

Don't repeat post the same images close together in time, it looks like your website is not current and you are recycling images because you don't have any new ones

Don't post only home listing, post some important value content to help buyers and sellers

Don't post bad home pictures

Don't post anything that will alienate your customers

Don't post anything that violates copyright laws

Don't post derogatory messages

Don't post swear or cuss words

Don't post bad language

Don't post misspellings and other typos, this is an English teacher's nightmare!

Don't post about your personal views for example politics. You run the risk of a large percentage of customers taking their money and spending it at a different business, most likely one of your competitors

BUSINESS VS PERSONAL

Your Business Social Media Networks vs Your Personal Social Media Networks

If you are the face of the company, be sure your personal social media is completely appropriate for your business. Once customers meet you, they might go search out your personal social media accounts.

2 SOCIAL MEDIA STATISTICS

FACEBOOK SOCIAL MEDIA STATISTICS

- 71% of American adults use Facebook, source https://blog.hootsuite.com/facebook-statistics/
- 74% of high income earners use Facebook, source https://blog.hootsuite.com/facebook-statistics/
- 74% of Facebook users log in daily, source https://blog.hootsuite.com/facebook-statistics/
- 90 million small businesses use Facebook, source

https://blog.hootsuite.com/facebook-statistics/

INSTAGRAM SOCIAL MEDIA STATISTICS

- 37% of American adults use Instagram, source https://blog.hootsuite.com/instagram-statistics/
- 11% of U.S. social media users shop on Instagam, source https://blog.hootsuite.com/instagram-statistics/
- 75.3% of U.S. businesses will use Instagram in 2020, source https://blog.hootsuite.com/instagram-statistics/

TWITTER SOCIAL MEDIA STATISTICS

- 22% of adults in the U.S. use Twitter, source https://blog.hootsuite.com/twitter-statistics/
- Tweets with hashtags gets 100% more engagement, source https://blog.hootsuite.com/twitter-statistics/

- 30 million of Twitter's daily users are American, source https://blog.hootsuite.com/twitter-statistics/

3 SOCIAL MEDIA CALENDAR

THE IMPORTANCE OF A SOCIAL MEDIA CALENDAR

The purpose of keeping a social media calendar is ...

You know when and what you are posting

You can prepare ahead of time for special dates or sales for your business

You can review to see if there were any changes in your sales and could the reason be related to any social media content you posted.

You can review historical data to decide going forward how you want to proceed.

You can review when you posted last year and if you want to change timing, content and networks you used

You can coordinate social media with other marketing goals and campaigns. By having a social media calendar, you can see ahead of time what is coming up for your business marketing plans. A social media calendar gives you time to think about and decide what you want to do.

Holidays and Days of Interest

Holidays

Special dates to post about

National days

Seasonality of your business

Birthdays and anniversaries of your business and team members

Plan out your marketing campaigns

Coordinate your social media with your website and other forms of marketing you use

There are many free and for a charge social media calendars available online. Find the one that works best for you and your business.

www.NationalDayCalendar.com

https://icalendars.net/celebrations/

Here is an example of a possible Social Media Calendar you can create on Excel. Create your own or locate one that works best for you.

Social Media Ideas for Real Estate

January 2020

February 2020

March 2020

Social Media Ideas for Real Estate

Social Media Ideas for Real Estate

Social Media Ideas for Real Estate

Social Media Ideas for Real Estate

4 CREATIVE POSTS

SOME POST EXAMPLES

🔥#JUSTLISTED 🏠♥️🏠

🚗🚗2 car garage

🛏 3 bedroom

🚽 3 bathrooms

🏠 great curb appeal 🎉

Call for more information

May Sell Real Estate Company

May.sell@REC.com

555-555-1212 call anytime

Add: Pictures of home below

Social Media Ideas for Real Estate

♡JUST LISTED ✹555 Patriot Way, America, US 55555 ✹3867sqft ✹ Listing Price $349,000 ❗

Add: Detail about home you listed

Please call or text me at 555-555-1212 📱 for more information!

Add: Pictures of home below

Non-MLS Listing - Located in Hickory Woods ♡♡♡

555 Winning Way, America, US 55555

Listed at $299,000

Add: Description of listing

Add: Pictures of home below

JUST SOLD

NOW AVAILABLE Great 4 BED 3 BATH home. Call me for a showing at 555-555-1212!

Close to 🏈 🏀 ⚽ 🏐 🎾 facilities and local schools

🏠OPEN HOUSE ☁️ ☔RAIN OR SHINE ❗

Join us tomorrow

Post Your Contact Information Based On Your Desired Frequency

Call/text/email us for more information –

(Your email address)

(your phone number)

5 INFORMATION FOR CLIENTS

WHAT SETS YOU APART IN YOUR LOCAL REAL ESTATE MARKET?

If you have any of the below items, make sure you post about it often so that anyone can access your information if they are viewing your social media networks. Also, chances are that they will share or tell others about your available information. Include the URL that links this content to the available information in your social media posts.

Downloads

Information you offer that is free or is available for a price

Checklists, articles, market statistics, and other materials that can be downloaded for free

Blog

Write a blog with content that clients or potential clients would benefit from and then link the blog in your post which shows you have credibility in the local market

Creative Content

Create creative content using an online graphics arts tool. Information could include tips, lists, timelines, and other quick and colorful information that catches the eye of clients or potential clients.

Newsletter

Your monthly newsletter

Seminars

Post when you will be offering Seminars

Seminar topics could be buying a home, selling a home, getting your home ready for sale

Other seminar topics could include speakers from other areas that clients could benefit such as trades like HVAC, closings, mortgage bankers, home inspection, etc.

eBooks

Create eBooks and have available on your website and link the URLs in your social media posts

Recommended eBooks for your clients and potential clients to help them become more knowledgeable which helps them when buying or selling

Videos

Post your own videos

Post videos of tours of your listings

Facebook Live for informational purposes

Podcast Channel

Your podcast

Your company podcast

Any recommended podcasts

YouTube Channel

A company or agent YouTube Channel. A company YouTube channel is a great way to set your business apart from your competition. As an agent, you can offer informative content. Information regarding the real estate market, community, relocation, and other areas of interest can inform possible potential clients are looking for an agent or real estate company to work with.

Additional Information

Other free materials

Post recommendations of accurate content to be read or watched to build goodwill and boost clients and potential clients knowledge in the real estate market

MARKETING

Plan your marketing strategy ahead of time. There are many email lists to get on in order to build your expertise and client base. The more you know, the greater your expertise becomes. You can pre-plan and schedule your emails ahead of time in order to make it super easy to have your marketing calendar all planned out well in advance. Write down what your aggressive multichannel marketing technique is and how you plan to implement it.

You can have a system to sending out emails to those on your email list. You want to add value each time you create an email. One idea would be:

1. Email valuable content
2. Email that asks for their business
3. Email your successes and testimonials you have received
4. Email what you can offer to them that adds value and helps them out

Possible Email Lists For You and Your Company To Get On

Email lists for things in your area such as national parks, free events, public places

Email lists for town and city notifications for example when alternate parking begins in winter

Email lists of county notifications for example where to

take the brush removed from your yard

Email lists for chamber of commerce events for example local festivals

Other Ideas

Find websites that have great content, locally, industry, and subject matter

Home Builders Association website

NARI website – National Association of Remodeling Inc.

New construction tours in neighborhoods

6 LISTINGS

Every agent and real estate company has their own style. Decide how you want your listings posted and go with that. You can always change your posting style depending on if it is working, new changes that evolve with posting options, or if you just want to change it up. Agents can vary the amount of detail in their posts such as a lot of the listing's detail, a few important points with the company phone number to contact, emojis, or other information in posts about the listing. In addition to the content you post, images are super important. This will catch the viewers eye and could lead someone to contact you so that they can see the property.

LISTING CONTENT IDEAS

Some Ideas Could Be ...

There are many ways to post your listings. You can add a lot of content, almost a paragraph, or you can add one or two lines more pointed in content. You must decide what the most important content is to include about the property for example bedrooms, bathrooms, neighborhood, age of building or mechanicals, or other points that customers are interested in. You can post your process or the next steps if someone is interested in seeing the property. Agents include their contact information in each, some, or no posts, it is your choice.

Some Headings You Could Begin Your Posting With

Just Listed!

>>>>>OPEN HOUSE ALERT<<<<<

Say hello to your new home!

A MUST SEE

OPEN HOUSE

#JUSTLISTED!

New Price

You can add symbols, shapes, and emojis within your posts. You can add captions on top of the images for emphasis.

IMAGES – IMAGES MATTER!!

IMPORTANT: The Quality of the Images of the Post Matters

Posting Images

Decide on the quantity of the images for the listing

Video tour of the listing

Birds-eye view of the listing

Rooms in the house

Front of house

Back of house

Pools

Waterfront property

Close up image of cool features for example a beautiful front door

Link your images to your website

Once you have your listing posted, there is other content you could post that parallels your listings

You could have a 4-step posting strategy to highlight your work and your sales ability:

Social Media Ideas for Real Estate

1. Just listed
2. Open house
3. Just Sold
4. Sold in X days

Congratulate your customers for example

"Congratulations to our Sellers"

"Congrats to our Buyers and Sellers"

Post if you list property and then sell it in a short time – 1 day or 1 week

Post your number of closings as the year progresses to show your effectiveness

Use words like "another" in your post, "Another home sold"

Do you have a client looking for a property? Post about that

Multiple images can be added to show all your listings/sales for a period of time

Image - Graphic Arts

Insert your logo in one of the corners in your posts

Add text over the main image

Phrases that can be imposed on top of the images

"Coming Soon"

"Just Listed"

"Open House"

"(Name of Neighborhood)"

"(Name of Subdivision)"

"Price Reduced"

Graphs or other statistical content using an online graphics tool

List of steps example "Steps to Writing an Offer"

List of top # tips

Images That Highlight The Area

Historic old photos of the area

Local beautiful areas

Local community assets

Local historic areas

Local parks

Local sunrises

Local sunsets

Other points of interest within a designated perimeter

PROPERTY VALUE

How much is my home worth. Describe how you value property. Link the URL if you have other information that someone can click to go to

How do you price your listings and decide on the fair market value

LISTING PROCESS

"How the Home Listing Process Works from Start to Finish", do you have a guide

Are your ready to sell your home

Tip(s) for listing your property

What you should remember to do before you sign on the dotted line

A list of things to do when you move to or from a home

Why Use An Agent VS Working On Your Own

Why should you hire an agent

Benefit of Using An Agent vs FSBO

Interview questions to ask a real estate agent

questions to ask before hiring a real estate agent

How to select the right agent.

What does a real estate agent do

What services you as an agent offer.

What you bring to the table as an agent which sets you apart from other agents

What is your marketing plan for buyers and sellers

Questions to ask your real estate agent

Questions to ask your real estate agent after ## days

Terminology and Purpose

Real estate knowledge

- CMA - Comparative marketing analysis
- MLS - Multiple listing service
- HOA - Home Owner Association
- Appraisal Company – What is it and what is their purpose
- Home Inspection Company – What is it and what is their purpose
- Title Company – What is it and what is their purpose
- Warranties – What are the different kinds and what is their purpose

Statistics: National Association of Realtors website for information and stats

BUYING

Buying A Home

Selecting an agent

Are you ready to buy a home

Are you financially ready to buy a home

Buying a home process

Best time to buy a house

Buying vs building

Cost of buying a home

Final Walkthrough: What to look for

Home buyers journey

Home buying mistakes

Home buying tips

House Hunting: What you need to know

How long does it take to buy a house

How much house can I afford

How the Home Buying Process works from start to finish

How to agree on the perfect home with your spouse

Social Media Ideas for Real Estate

How to budget for a new home

How to buy a home

How to buy a home that will increase in value over time

How to buy and sell a home at the same time

How to find your perfect home online

How to learn your neighborhood, research the neighborhood

How to make an offer on a house

Investing in vacation rental property

Make a list of what you want in a new home in order of importance

Make a list of what you want to avoid in a new home in order of importance

Negotiating price

Searching online

Things buyers should not forget to do when buying a home

Things to consider before purchasing a new home

Upfront costs to buying a home, how much to budget for

Upkeep things you may not have thought about

What are "contingencies" in real estate

What does the Housing Market look like where you are buying

What is the process once I submit an offer to purchase

What paperwork do you need to have ready

What to do if your home purchase falls through

What to know before buying a home

What you need to know about the home you are buying: property taxes, utilities, fees

What's the difference between Certified Homebuyer or Mortgage Preapproval

When buying a home, what can you negotiate

First Time Home Buyers

First time home buyer considerations

First time home buyer check list

First time home buyer guide – create your own guide for your clients

Tips for first time home buyer

To Do List for first time home buyer

Down Payment Information

Do you really need a down payment when buying a home

Down payment tips

How to save for a Down Payment on your first or next house

What to Consider When Looking to Buy Property

Are you buying this year or next year

Single Family House vs Condominium vs Townhouse

Content involved when buying property

- Your credit score
- A down payment
- Set your budget
- Getting pre-approved loans
- Calling an agent
- Insurance quote for the property

What is a Condominium

What is a Townhome

Condo vs Townhome: What's the difference

Condominium vs Townhome: What costs are involved

What is a Home Owner Association

What is included in Home Owner Association fees

What is not included in Home Owner Association fees

How much are the Home Owner Association Fees in different areas

SELLING

Selling A Home

How to sell a house

Selling a home process

Best time to sell your house

Insider Tips

Sellers Tips

A Practical Step-by-Step Home Selling Guide – create your own guide for your clients

Are you ready to sell your home. Home checklist – take this quiz and find out

Common home-selling mistakes

Common mistakes sellers make by ignoring home improvements

Social Media Ideas for Real Estate

Does home staging work

Easy steps to determine what your home is worth

Gardening tips to keep your house curb appeal before selling

Home Sellers Journey

"How the Home Selling Process Works from Start to Finish" – create your own client guide

How to boost your home's value for very little money

How to make more money selling your home

How to put together marketing materials for potential buyers

How to prepare your home for an appraisal

How to prepare your home for sale if you have inside or outside pets

How to prepare your Kitchen for sale

How to get your home "home showing ready"

How to get your home "Open House ready"

How to sell a home

How to sell and buy a home at the same time

How to stage a house that sells

Making improvements to sell your home

No-cost tips to sell your home faster

Popular home renovations

Reasons why your home may not be selling

Selling an inherited home

Selling your home during the spring

Selling your home during the summer

Selling your home during the fall

Selling your home during the winter

Should you complete home renovations DIY or hire a professional

Smells home buyers hate

Successful home sale tips

Tips for selling your home faster

Tips for faster sale for example bury a statue of St Joseph upside down in your yard

Tip bake bread in your oven before an open house (but don't burn it, start with a clean oven)

Tips for curb appeal

Tips for selling your home in the spring

Tips for selling your home in the summer

Tips for selling your home in the fall

Tips for selling your home in the winter

- Tips for staging a house
- Thinking about selling: What buyers are looking for in a home
- Think like a buyer when selling your home
- Upfront costs to selling a home, what to budget for
- Want to get the most money from the sale of your home? Follow these steps ...
- Ways to get your home sold faster
- Ways to increase your number of home showings
- What does the Housing Market look like where you are selling
- What is a Home Warranty
- What is a "Sellers Disclosure"
- What is the process once I submit an offer to purchase
- What paperwork do you need to have ready
- What to do if your home sale falls through
- What to know before selling a home
- What you need to do to get your home ready for sale
- What to remove in order to avoid offending potential buyers
- When to start working on your house in order to sell it in the future

What can you do to help sell your home faster

Which updates do home buyers want

Why is your house not selling

For Sale By Owner

For sale by owner: What can an agent offer

Reasons why a For Sale By Owner is a bad idea

What is involved in a For Sale By Owner

Mechanicals In Your Home

How long do mechanicals last on average before replacement is recommended for example roof, windows, furnace, water heater, etc.

Should you require replacement of mechanicals before you buy the house

OPEN HOUSE

When and where your Open House(s) is/are

"Must see Open Houses this weekend"

What is your listings Open House Process

To Do List to get your house ready for an Open House

To Do List of what consider when going to an Open House

Why sellers should leave during the open house and showings

Does your blog include your open houses. Is it linked in your posts

WRITING THE OFFER

Process

Negotiation

What to include and what to leave out

Pitfalls

Active option contract

Cash offers

Contingency tips

Down payment money and closing costs

Earnest money

What are closing costs

What are "contingencies" in real estate

What are the costs associated with writing the offer

What are the costs associated with the down payment

What are the costs associated with the appraisal

What are the costs associated with the home inspection

What are the costs associated with the credit report

What are the costs associated with the homeowners insurance

What is Earnest Money

LOANS and MORTGAGE

What is a mortgage

What is a second mortgage

What type of mortgage is best for you

Credit score

Debt-to-Income Ratio

Social Media Ideas for Real Estate

Down payment tips and information

Easy ways to pay off your mortgage early

Frequently asked mortgage questions from buyers

How do certain loans work

How much do you need for a Down Payment

How much does a home appraisal cost

How much home can I really afford

How lower interest rates could affect you

How raising interest rates could affect you

How to get a mortgage

How to get a mortgage if you are self-employed

How to get a mortgage with a ### credit score

How to get a mortgage with no credit score

Land Contract

Mortgage options to avoid

Mortgage Prequalification vs Preapproval

Preapproval explanation

Prequalification explanation

Property taxes and your mortgage

Refinancing

Talking with a banker

Tips for a mortgage approval

Title Insurance

To Do List

Top # mortgage question and their answers

Types of Home Loans, pros and cons

VA loans

What does a home appraisal cover

What are Mortgage Points

What are the different kinds of mortgage lenders

What is a Down Payment
What is a 15-Year mortgage

What is a 30-Year mortgage

What is a 15-Year Fixed-Rate mortgage

What is a 30-Year Fixed-Rate mortgage

What is an Adjustable Rate Mortgage (ARM)

What is a Conventional Loan

What is a FHA Loan

What is a Subprime Mortgage

What is a VA Loan

What is Escrow

What is Private Mortgage Insurance (PMI)

What is the average monthly mortgage payment

What is the mortgage process, how long does it take

What is the Mortgage Underwriting Process

What do you need to be preapproved

What's included in a monthly mortgage payment

What's the difference between a preapproval vs a prequalification

When do you know you are 'Mortgage Ready'

HOME INSPECTION

What it is

How to prepare for it

Major repair issues to prevent your purchase

Major repair issues to prevent your sale

How does an inspection report differ for the seller vs the buyer

How to choose a home inspector

What does a home inspection inspect

What does a home inspector look for

REAL ESTATE CLOSING

Process

Common mistakes to avoid

Legal Documents

Money required

Tips

Tips for same day buying and selling

What are Closing Costs

What is needed

What to do after the closing is complete, follow up

What to expect

MOVING

Moving day cheat sheet

Tips for moving day

Tips for moving same day when you sell and buy a home

Transition Experts

Transition Lists

What costs are involved when you move

HOMEOWNERS INSURANCE

What is homeowner's insurance

What does homeowner's insurance cover

VALUATION OF PROPERTY

What is the value of the different rooms in a house

How to value the materials in your kitchen and other rooms in your house

How to value garages, carports, and converted garages

How to value lake front property

How to value a house with a pool in your real estate market

Are condos a good investment

BUILDING A HOUSE VS BUYING AN ALREADY BUILT HOUSE

Buying land

Costs

Permits

Upgrades that will pay back

Value of a house you are considering purchasing vs building a new home

7 TIPS

Posting tips is an excellent way to give great content and encourage repeat visits to your social media networks. If you have clients and potential clients, this is content they are looking for or may have not considered. In addition, this gives the impression that you are an expert in this industry.

BUYING TIPS

Buyers Tips

Tips for buyers

Things to do to avoid ...

Things to consider before buying a home

Reasons why you should use an agent

Reasons to buy a house this spring

Reasons to buy a house this summer

Reasons to buy a house this fall

Reasons to buy a house this winter

Things to do to get ready to buy a home

A tip for a successful home purchase

Home buying tip

Tips for house hunting

Tips for Millennial Homebuyers

Tips to get ready to buy a home

Did you know ...

One mistake to avoid when ....

Biggest mistakes buyers make

Common mistakes buyers make

Personal budget before buying a home, how to get ready

First time home buying tips

Tips for first time home buyers

First time home buyer mistakes

How home ownership is an investment

How home ownership is more beneficial than renting

SELLING TIPS

Sellers tips

Tips for sellers

A tip for home sellers

A tip for a successful home sale

Reasons why you should use an agent

Things to consider when thinking of selling your home

Things to consider selling and moving to a new area

Things to do to avoid ...

Social Media Ideas for Real Estate

\# Best renovations that pay off

\# Biggest mistakes sellers make

\# Biggest mistakes home owners make

\# Biggest overpricing mistakes

Can you add value by increasing room purpose for example renovating the attic into a bedroom

Common mistakes sellers make

\# Curb appeal tips

\# Important tips for home images

Listing photo tips

Mistakes first time home owners may make

One mistake to avoid when ...

Real estate tips

\# Staging tips

\# Tips for a quick spring sale

\# Tips for a quick summer sale

\# Tips for a quick fall sale

\# Tips for a quick winter sale

Tips to list your home this spring

Tips to list your home this summer

Social Media Ideas for Real Estate

Tips to list your home this fall

Tips to list your home this winter

Tips to help you get your home ready for sale

Tips to increase your home's value

What to do to get your home ready for sale before calling an agent

Ways to get your home sold faster

Ways to get your house ready for sale

Did you know ...

Design tips: Kitchen design tips

Design tips: Garage Design Tips

Design tips: Family room design tips

Design tips: How to make a small bathroom look bigger

Design tips: Backyard

Design tips: Landscape

Landscaping tips to get the best curb appeal

Simple things you can do to make your house look more inviting

How to make your home more appealing to buyers

CLOSING TIPS

Understanding closing costs

Use an online graphics tool to create tips to post

Things a title company does when buying a home

Things a title company does when selling a home

MOVING TIPS

How to save money on moving costs

How to prepare for a cross country move

HOME OWNERSHIP TIPS

Mindless home habits that are costing you money

Reasons to invest in quality roofing, plumbing, and electrical systems

Tips for smart homes

Things to do to maintain your furnace

Things to do to switch your home from winter to spring

Things to do to switch your home from spring to

winter

Things you need to pay for when you own a home

Tips for your lawn mower

Tips for your snow blower

Unexpected costs you might incur with home ownership

Avoid these common DIY mistakes

Best home improvements that will increase your home's value

Boost your home's value with paint

Budget friendly ideas to make your house look expensive

Can fixing up your home affect your taxes

Curb appeal tips

Hacks to tackle your fall cleaning checklist in minutes

Hacks to tackle your spring cleaning checklist in minutes

Home maintenance chores

How to be smart with your money ahead of a home improvement

How to get your home ready for….
How to prepare your home for ….

How to make your mechanicals last longer

- How to overseed your lawn

- Kitchen remodeling on a budget

- Seasonal home maintenance tasks to tackle

- Smart garage storage

- Sustainable renovations

- Time for maintenance

- Top # bathroom design and remodeling trends

- Upgrades that pay for themselves, ie furnace, water-faucets, toilets,

- Window washing tips

Companies You Can Partner With To Generate Sales

Partner with these types of companies to build expertise or to recommend when clients need a contractor to get their home ready for sale with you as their agent. You will be your client's best friend if you have great trades companies!

Deck

Electrician

Flooring

Handyman

HVAC

Lawn care

Painters

Plumber

Pool

Roofing

Snow removal

Window replacement

8 CONTENT POSTING

Sometimes you might be looking for some interesting information that brings clients and potential clients to your social media networks. If your goal is repeat visits, here are some ideas of other real estate related content to post about. Also, some the ideas below add to your expertise and can set you apart from your competition.

CLIENT CONTENT

Another Happy Client

Best real estate advice from realtor.com

Best time to do certain things to homes ie change batteries in smoke detectors

Can houseplants clean the air

Changes in local or area property statistics

Countertop materials

Designing a Wine Room

Downsizing

Effect of staging your home on your sale price

Flat-Fee Real Estate Agent

Home maintenance tips for spring

Home maintenance tips for summer

Home maintenance tips for fall

Home maintenance tips for winter

House odors, mold, water, smoke, pets

How do pools affect the value of selling and buying a home, in different parts of the country

Insist on a Home Inspection

Is a bigger house within your budget

Social Media Ideas for Real Estate

Know what you want vs what you need in your dream home

Local Market Statistics – you could use an online-graphics tool for a great image

Outdoor décor to transform your backyard

Painted cabinets vs stained

Pictures of your office, info about your staff

Rental Property Investment

Smart home technology

Solar panels

Tips to creating … (house related)

Tips to help your pets during fireworks

Turning your garage into a luxury garage

Wallpaper vs paint

What to budget for home ownership – First time home buyers

What to consider when transitioning from renting to buying

Why home ownership is an investment

Why your neighbor's home sold and yours did not

LOCATION, LOCATION, LOCATION

Important Locations That Highlight Your Listing's Area

How are the communities changing for example new businesses, new schools, new roads

Important locations for property buyers

Titles of locations for example "Wisconsin Dells – The Waterpark Capital of the World"

Valuable community assets including carnivals, community events, fairs, local bands, parades, auto shows, kids events, children's museums, dog parks

What is within walking, driving or near to distance for example freeways, schools, community locations, shopping

Awards

Awards your community wins

Did your state make any Top 10 Lists that benefit your real estate market

Your areas "Top" locations for example Dallas's top public swimming pools

More Informative Location Content

Amenities in the area

Area real estate statistics

Best free things to do in your community

Best schools

Businesses coming to your real estate market: ABC Company to bring 400 new jobs to the area

Fall leaf color changing calendar

Go Explore

Great places to get a cup of coffee in the area

Hidden gems in your community, business that have been around many years – decades

Historic buildings in your community

20## Home prices: What you need to know

Housing trends and shifts in this year

Internet – broadband, satellite, streaming

Local restaurant recommendations

Local sports schedules

Market overview of property – market statistics

Monthly local housing stats

Monthly Calendar of Events for the Month in your

Social Media Ideas for Real Estate

city/county

Parks in your area

Pet friendly areas with pet positive locations and events

Pool vs no pool

Real Estate Market News: Your state or local area

Relocation

School reports

Sky- Events in the sky in your area ie blood moon, eclipse, shooting stars

Sports teams

Things to do in the area

Town hall meetings that affect your market for your customers to attend if they are interested

Water front property information

What is located near your listings that buyers may be interested in

What is the real estate market like in your area for buyers

What is the real estate market like in your area for sellers

What makes this area special

What do to in the area

Why you will love this area

9 YOUR BUSINESS

Your Current Business

Post your listings

Post when you have business "Under Contract"

Post your sales

Post your Open Houses

Post your Mission Statement

Add your phone number so potential customers can contact you

Add your website URL in your posts

We appreciate your business post

Have more questions about …? Call me at 555-555-1212 or visit my website!

Your business's sales record over the years

FREE Home Valuation, wondering what your home is worth?

Post that you have a client looking for a particular home or in a neighborhood

The company's anniversary

The company's birthday

** Ask for the business "Call me if you are thinking of buying or selling"

Your Quality of Work

Ask for the sale: Getting ready to move? Please call me at ...

Awards you or your company received

Benefits of using a real estate agent, what you can do for them

Conferences you attended ie National Association of Realtors Conference

Congratulations about your closings with new owners

Did any clients give you a gift? Possibly post with the image of the gift

Social Media Ideas for Real Estate

Difference between websites like Zillow.com and local realtor websites

Do you have a specialty area of real estate Ie investment real estate or a neighborhood expert

Do you thank your customers after the sale? Host a Seller Customer Appreciation Event

Do you thank your customers after the sale? Host a Buyer Customer Appreciation Event

Fundamentals of your real estate customer service program

How do you research the local market

How many years have you been in business. Post if it is substantial.

Post about awards you receive including the photo of you holding your award

Public transportation statistics, facts, and if houses sell better around public transportation

Screen shot of your rating on your Facebook page

Testimonials, post with permission

What education do you have. Post about additional training when you add more

Your anniversary of number of years in real estate

Your anniversary at that company

Your recommendations to sell a home on a tight

timeline

Your success rate

About You

Keep in mind how visitors will view what you post. The goal is to grow your business, not reduce it.

About Me Post, link it back to your blog

Any personal awards, not business related

Charities you support

Do you have an Agent Scorecard

Maybe do not post your birthday – too much information for security reasons

Post any high review ratings you receive

Volunteering you do

What is happening in your life

Who You Work With

Additions to your Team

Welcome post of new staff who joined the organization

Is your business hiring agents and other staff

Your staff's volunteering programs, things they are involved in

Images

Photos of your listing

Images of your office staff

Images of your office meetings

Link your images to your website

When you are at conferences, association meetings, or getting certifications

You and your customers holding a Sold or Just Listed Sign in front of the listing

Link Content Reflective Of Your Expertise

Changes in laws: local, county, or state changes, upcoming public hearings

Do you have a blog which you can link to your blog in your social media networks

Don't sell your home alone – use an agent

Earn more by using an agent

Explain difference between Market Value vs Market Price

Myths about real estate agents

Plan for finding the perfect home for your client

Plan for selling your client's home

Real Estate Terminology

20## Real Estate Trends

Relocation services

Should you use your friend or relative as your real estate agent

Transition experts: your company information of how to transition living location

Why hire a single agent vs a team

Why hire a team vs a single agent

PHRASES

Another ...

Are you ready to ...

Crucial Tips ...

Do's and Dont's

Expert

Get in the Holiday Spirit

How to Maximize your ...

Important Tips ...

Landscape Beauty

Luxury home

Meal Prep Fun

Motivated Seller

Myths

New Listing Alert

Positively Beaming

Process ...

Pros and Cons of ...

Remodeled Home

Steps ...

Take your home to the next level

Top # Ways ...

We love this community!!

What you need to know

What's included in

What's the difference?

What's the difference between

Days Of The Week

Happy Monday

Monday motivation

Tuesday Tip(s)

Throwback Thursday

Happy Friday, TGIF

Happy Saturday

Super Saturday

Simple Saturday

Selfie Saturday

Selfie Sunday

Good Morning Sunday

Weekend!

New Year New Home?

BUYING INVESTMENT PROPERTY

What you need to know

Pitfalls

Recommendations

Tips

FLIPPING A HOME

What is home flipping

How to flip a home

Pitfalls

Recommendations

Tips

What you need to know

SMART HOMES

What products are available

Your listings with smart home equipment installed

Wi-fi enabled electrical plugs

Does this bring value to your home

10 ENGAGEMENT

Another way to encourage visitors to your social media networks is by asking questions. Keep in mind, if you ask a question, you might need to take the time to reply back in a timely manner. It is a great way to get the "Locals" to engage and for folks from a distance away to get recommendations.

POST CONVERSATIONS THAT ENGAGE

Are you ready for …? Snow, spring flowers, mowing the lawn

Best brunch restaurants?

Best business to visit?

Best drink at your favorite coffee shop?

Best Foodie Restaurant?

Best restaurant to watch sporting events at is …

Does your family like to …?

How do you relax?

What is a great activity you participate in around here?

What is the most romantic restaurant in the area?

What is your favorite local restaurant?

What traditions do you have …?

What type of floor plan do you prefer?

What's your favorite restaurant in this community?

Where can you go as a couple? As a family? With kids?

Would you prefer to eat x or y? For example stuffing or mashed potatoes at Thanksgiving

11 RESOURCE WEBSITES

WEBSITES WITH GREAT CONTENT FOR YOUR POSTS

Here are some great websites with interesting content

- http://www.amazinginteriordesign.com/
- https://www.bhg.com/
- https://www.houzz.com/
- https://www.imagineyourhouse.com/
- https://www.investopedia.com/
- https://www.lightingtutor.com/
- https://magazine.realtor/
- https://www.marthastewart.com/
- https://www.nar.realtor/about-nar
- https://www.opentable.com/start/home
- https://www.realtor.com/
- https://www.simplifyingthemarket.com/en/

Social Media Ideas for Real Estate

- https://www.zillow.com/

- (Your local media).com
- (state)realestate.com
- state)realtors.org   for example floridarealtors.org
- http://www.trendinghomenews.com/
- Search for Housing Market Statistics Websites

- https://emojipedia.org/
- https://getemoji.com/

12 MORE CONTENT IDEAS

OTHER IDEAS FOR CONTENT TO POST

Your Community

Annual charity events in your community

Area dining opportunities, create your own list or find links you can use

Best things to do in (your city) this weekend

Create your own video to highlight what's great about the community

Drawings of proposals ie schools, community buildings, public transportation

Easter egg hunt

Facebook neighborhood community groups

Social Media Ideas for Real Estate

Free admission to events in your area at certain times throughout the year

Fun runs in your community

fun things to do in ... (your town)

Monthly – Events calendar for (your city) – "November 20## Events Calendar for Chicago"

News articles: tax bills that are incorrect, upcoming detours

Openings of new businesses, grocery stores, post office, malls, schools, restaurants

Organizations in your area that are fundraising, sponsoring charities, ie school supplies for kids

Parade videos (Homecoming parades, 4th of July parades)

Phone videos of things happening in your area ie tree lighting, 5K run winners, sporting events

Restaurants great for outdoor dining in xxx(Chicago) opentable.com

Special deals in your community

Taste of (your city) for example, The Taste of Chicago

What's going on at other local businesses for example Lions Club Nuts Sale stand

creative Money-Saving Household Hacks

smart holiday shopping tips

Social Media Ideas for Real Estate

\# springtime drinks

\# summer drinks

\# fall drinks

\# winter drinks

Accolades company

Buy now or wait

\# Cable alternatives to save you money

Charity Awareness Month

Chili Cook-off for charity

Decorating: # excellent decorating apps

Ease into spring

Ease into summer

Ease into fall

Ease into winter

Foundations you support

Funny home articles and your sense of humor

Garage Sale Season

Goals to improving your home

Hacks to save money around the house, ways to save money around the house, tips to ...

Social Media Ideas for Real Estate

Historic vs New: Which home is best for you

Home maintenance seasonal checklist

Home Projects: Which can I DIY

Home Trends

Holiday decoration ideas

Holiday recipes

Homemade things to make

Hospitality How-tos

Household hacks

How to add a chalkboard by using chalkboard paint

How to build equity in your home

How to lower your electric bill

Images to go with national days

Images of beautiful places around your town, historic places

Benefits of Instagram stories for your business (for your industry or other businesses)

Interest rate information

Is this year the year you will reach your home (ownership, moving, downsizing) dreams

Kitchen backsplashes

Social Media Ideas for Real Estate

Landscape

New year new trends

Pet images

Post about you and your family if you want

Post your weekly meetings

Prevent frozen pipes

Quotes

Real cost of renting

Recipes

Replace or Reface your cabinets

Schools: 5 reasons school ratings matter

Seasonal changes – Fall is here, Spring is here,

Short videos of other content you find interesting,

Should you turn your home into a rental?

Tailgate for a Cause

Ways to save money

Websites with great content ideas, work related, and fun ideas

Welcoming sports figures who join local teams ie NFL new players

What kind of XXX are you (holiday shopper)

What room should you remodel first or if at all

What to look for in a home remodeling contractor

What's happening this weekend: in local areas ie year round ideas, #(town location subject)

When to plant spring flowers

Why pet friendly homes are desired

13 # HASHTAGS

#Hashtags

Hashtags can help your posts get found at a subject related central spot. If someone is looking for a house to purchase, they may be following a particular hashtag on a social media network and then they may discover you. The goal with social media hashtags is that potential clients will begin following your specific social media posts because they like your content. People who are following that hashtag on the social media channel will see your post or share it with a friend.

However, always check the hashtag before using it. Sometimes a particular hashtag may not be currently used or it may have content that does not reflect your business goals.

PERSONALIZED HASHTAGS

#(your company name)

#(agent name)

#(your city name)

#(your state name)

#(your neighborhood)

#(city)realtors

#(state)HomesForSale

#(state)realtors

#(state)RealEstate

#(realtors)

#(your name)realestate

#((your city)realestate

#(your city)realestateagent

#(neighborhood)

#(neighborhood)homesforsale

Social Media Ideas for Real Estate

#(state)homesforsale

#buyin(neighborhood)

#modernhomesof(city)

#sell(city,neighborhood)

#(X)suburbs

#(X)market

#(state)homes

#(state)LocalRealtor

#soldby(your name)

#(the listing number)

#ask(your name)

#ask(your company)

#trust(your company)

REAL ESTATE RELATED HASHTAGS

#approved

#builders

#BuyAHome

#cashoffers

#charm

#closingtime

#comingsoon

#contractors

#cashoffers

#COMINGSOON

#condosforsale

#contractors

#customhomes

#dreams

#dreamhomes

Social Media Ideas for Real Estate

#emptynest

#estate

#expert

#familyhome

#farmhousechic

#financing

#FORRENT

#FORSALE!

#greathome

#homecheck

#homeownership

#home

#homes

#honmesforsale

#homeflipping

#homesecurity

#homesweethome

#HouseExpert

#househunting

#housesforsale

#housing

#industryleader

#invest

#investinrealestate

#investment

#JustClosed

#JUSTLISTED!

#JUSTSOLD

#LISTED

#listing

#listingilove

#location

Social Media Ideas for Real Estate

#locationlocationlocation

#LowMortgageRates

#luxuryhomes

#luxuryhomemarketingspecialist

#makeanoffer

#markettrends

#mortgage

#MortgageRates

#neighborhoodamenities

#newconstruction

#newhome

#newhouse

#newlisting

#NEWPRICE!

#OPENHOUSE

#preapproval

Social Media Ideas for Real Estate

#pricedrop

#property

#quicktip

#realtor

#realestate

#realestateagents

#realestateexpert

#realestateforsale

#referral

#refinance

#relocation

#relocationexpert

#relocationspecialist

#renovated

#sell

#showings

Social Media Ideas for Real Estate

#suburbs

#testimonialtuesday

#SOLD

#topagent

#wegotthejobdone

DAYS OF THE WEEK HASHTAGS

#Monday (s)

#HappyMonday

#MondayMorning

#MondayMotivation

#Tuesday (s)

#Wednesday (s)

#Thursday (s)

#ThrowbackThursday

#Friday (s)

#Saturday (s)

#Sunday (s)

#SundayThoughts

#Weekend

#GoodMorning

INTERESTING

Funny Personal Story

I was at a college orientation with one of my kids. Every parent and student were sitting at tables with name tags on. During the breaks, my LinkedIn searches sky rocketed with people looking me up. I thought it was kind of funny that I did not even know these folks but they were curious about me. So be aware of your 'social media surroundings'.

About the Author

Danielle McCorkle has worked in social media for a number of years. She has posted on many social media networks for different companies. As a manager of eCommerce, her experience includes managing and sometimes setting up ecommerce sites Amazon.com, Walmart.com, Jet.com, eBay.com and other eCommerce sites. In addition, the author has used search term programs, managed marketing campaigns, and worked with other social media companies. She received a Bachelor's of Science – Retail Degree from the University of Wisconsin-Madison.